SERGE MONAST

THE TORONTO PROTOCOLS

6.6.6.

SERGE MONAST

THE TORONTO PROTOCOLS

6.6.6.

Serge Monast (1945-1996) ©

Original title : *Le Protocole de Toronto : 6.6.6. Québec année zéro. Deux documents inédits : « Panem et circenses » et « L'aurore rouge »* [Murmures d'Irem, nr.7] (1995).

Cover : Ethos

Translation : Omar Filali

Éditions Ethos ®
www.editionsethos.com
contact@editionsethos.com

ISBN : 978-84-19006-64-6

Legal deposit : July 1, 2023

 Serge Monast (1945-1996) was a Canadian investigative journalist, poet and essayist. He is known to English-speaking readers mainly for Blue Beam Project. He was an active member of the Social Credit Party of Canada. In the early 1990s, he started writing on the theme of the New World Order and conspiracies hatched by secret societies, being particularly inspired by the works of William Guy Carr. He founded the International Free Press Agency (AIPL – Agence Internationale de Presse libre), where he published most of his work on these themes, achieving some prominence with an interview on esotericist and ufologist Richard Glenn's TV show "Ésotérisme Expérimental", in which he repeatedly warned his audience about the dangers of a World Government. In 1994, he published "Le Projet Blue Beam" ("Blue Beam project"), in which he detailed his claim that NASA, with the help of the United Nations, was attempting to implement a New Age religion with the Antichrist at its head and start a New World Order, via a technologically simulated Second Coming of Christ. He also gave talks on this topic. In 1995, he published his most detailed work, "Les Protocoles de Toronto (6.6.6)", modelled upon "The Protocols of the Elders of Zion", wherein he said a Masonic group called "6.6.6" had, for twenty years, been gathering the world's powerful to establish the New World Order and control the minds of individuals. By 1995 and 1996, Monast said he was being hunted by the police and authorities for involvement in "networks of prohibited information". He died of a heart attack in his home in December 1996, at age 51, the day after being arrested and spending a night in jail, under very strange and suspicious conditions.

AUTHOR'S NOTE

End of June 1967: in Montreal there is Expo 67; in Ottawa, there are the final preparations for the "Centenary of the Confederation"; in the U.S it is the challenge of the Vietnam War and, through the country, the "Flower Power". We are close to the events of May 1968 in France, the explosion of nationalism in Quebec, the Woodstock Festival in the U.S... But at the same time, the end of June 1967 marks the final preparations for the development of the Plan of the "Fall of Nations" by the highest levels of Anglo-Saxon Freemasonry in Toronto (Canada).

This secret meeting, highly "Confidential", is organized by the "6.6.6." (so they call themselves), that is, those who run the 6 largest banks in the world, the 6 largest energy consortia on the planet (including the oil part), and the 6 largest consortia of agri-food (which includes the control of the main Food Roads of the World).

These 6.6.6., being the most senior international financiers, will define, within their meeting, a "Common Strategy" for absolute control over "World Trade"; on the possession of the Energy Weapon (the open gateway of the twenty-first century); and the international control of the food (which also includes, for them, the pharmaceutical companies which include, in turn, the global market for "Vitamins" and "vaccines").

Their "plan" boils down to three major themes: The Economic, the Political, and the Social Policy for the 70's and 80's. If successful, it must inevitably lead to the capture of "Global Power" by implementing the "New World Order", the same which U.S President George Bush will do much to promote in the early 90s.

The Title of the Document of the 6.6.6: "PANEM and circuses" (From Bread and Circus Games) [i.e. an old Roman phrase to describe how the Emperors used to entertain and feed the masses so that they would be distracted from taking an interest in politics].

BREAD AND CIRCUS[1]

[The document: *Bread and Circus*. Globalist Project Goal: The "Vital Genocide for the benefit of the hidden Profit". Project Financing means: Among other things, use of Humanitarian Aid, International Food Aid to fund the "Multinationals" of the 6.6.6.]

The document:

All the historic periods having led to the decline of civilizations were quite marked, without exception, by "the Spirit of the Wandering people". Today, we have to make so that this "Spirit" is translated by a "World Society of the Leisure" under all its forms. This "Leisure" has to consist of the [Sex], of the [Drugs], of the [Sport], of the [Travel and Exoticism], and [Leisure activities] in general, but accessible to all the sectors of society. The Man has to manage to believe that it is "Modern", and that his modernity consists of his capacity, and his possibility of being able to enjoy much, and now all which surrounds him.

---

1   *Panem et Circenses* (1967). (Editor's note.)

To achieve this objective it is imperative to be able to infiltrate the Medias (radio, television, newspapers), settings of "Fashion" and "Culture" (circles of New Music) by which we will influence, for sure all the layers of Western Societies. Thus taking under the control of the "Senses" the youth (tomorrow's adults), we will have consequently the way clear for infiltrating and transform in depth without being disturbed, the Politics, and the Legal System and the Education and thus allowing us to radically change the course, the future direction of Societies covered by our "Plan".

The populations, we know it, do not have any historical memory. They tirelessly repeat mistakes of the past without realizing that these mistakes had driven their forefathers before them, to the same forfeitures as they will live for the worse before the end of this century. See, for example, that their grandfathers had lived at the beginning of this century thanks to the relentless work of our predecessors.

After having experienced, without limitation, the liberation of the morals, the abolition of the morality (in other words, the wandering of the spirit), they experienced the "Economic Crisis" and then the "War". Today, their grandchildren and their children will go straight to an outcome similar, even worse because this time, he will finally allow us to establish our "New World Order" but none of them are able to realize this, they will all be too preoccupied to excessively satisfy their most primary sensual needs.

A "standard" generally more important, and that has already proven itself at the beginning of this century in the construction and implementation of the [Communist system] by the late-lamented Senior Officers of our lodges is the profitability of "the Exception". In principle, we know the Exception proves the General rule that is contrary to it. But in our vocabulary, it is the Exception that should be imposed to all. We need to make sure to make "Exceptions" in different spheres of the Society, as being new "Rules" applicable to all conditions, a primary objective of all the future social protests carried out by the Nations Youth.

Thus exception will become the fuse by which all the historical society will collapse on itself in shortness of breath and an unprecedented confusion.

The foundations of the "Western Society"in their essence, originate in a straight line from the Judeo-Christian heritage. It is precisely this same heritage which made of "Family", the "Node", the "Cornerstone" of all existing social structure. Our predecessors who had financed the revolutionary writers of the late nineteenth century and early twentieth century had understood the importance to divide, then to shatter the "vital Nucleus" if they wanted to, in Russia, to succeed in setting up the new "Communist System" at that time.

And that is precisely what they did by making meticulously produced by nonconformist philosophers and writers at the time: "A Manifesto to the glory of the God-State", which shall have the absolute priority on the individual, on the "Family".

To end with certainty in the construction of a World Government, [A New Community World Order] where all the individuals, without exception, will be subjected to the "World State" of the "New Order", we have to, first of all, remove the "Family" (what will entail, at the same moment, the disappearance of the ancestral religious teachings), and in the second place, level all the individuals by removing "Social classes", in particular, "Middle classes". But we have to proceed in such a way that all these changes appear as arising from the popular will; that they have the appearance of the "Democracy".

In using isolated cases, but amplifying them to the extreme with the help of student protests infiltrated by us, journalists favorable to our cause and politicians purchased, we will be able to put in place new organizations having all the appearances of the "Modernity" as an "Office of Child Protection" protected by a "Charter of Rights and Freedoms".

For the success of our "World Plan: [The Red Plan]", it is necessary us to make implant in all the Western Societies of the

70's, "Offices for the Protection of Children" among which the officials (of young intellectuals without experience, freshly out of Universities where are highlighted our internationalist principles), will comply literally, without proper judgment, the "Charter of the Rights of the Child". Who will dare to oppose this without being identified at the same time with the barbarians of the Middle Ages?

This "Charter" painstakingly developed in our "Lodges", we will finally eliminate any parental authority in the family by shattering people fiercely opposed to one another for the protection of their personal interests. It will encourage children to denounce parents very authoritarian because too traditional, too religious. It will contribute thus to subjecting parents to a "Collective Psychosis of Fear", which inevitably will cause, in a general way in society, a relaxation of parental authority. Thus we shall have succeeded in the first instance, to produce a society similar to that of Russia of the 50's where the children denounced their parents to the State, and this without anyone noticing.

Thereby transferring to the State the "Parental Role", it will be much easier thereafter, of us to monopolize, one by one, all the responsibilities that had been, until to date, the exclusive responsibility of the parents. This is how we can make be considered by all as an abuse against children, the traditional religious education of the Judeo-Christian origin.

In the same time, but at another level, we shall make register in the highest Laws of the Nations, than all the Religions, the Worship and the religious Practices of any kind, including the "Witchcraft and the Magic" must all be respected in the same way as the others.

This will then be of a disconcerting ease than to transfer this role of the state in relation to the child to the highest international bodies such as the United Nations.

Understand this well: "Our goal is not to protect children, or anyone from another, but to cause the collapse and subsequent fall of Nations which are a major obstacle to the implementation of our "New World Order". That is why the "Office of Child Protection" must be invested with absolute legal authority. They must be able, as they see fit, but always under the pretext of protecting the child, to remove them from their original home environments and place them in family backgrounds or foreign government centers that have been established for our internationalist principles and religions. Therefore, it will complete the final breaking of the "Western Family Unit". For without the protection and monitoring of their original parents, these children will be permanently handicapped in their psychological and moral development, and consequently represent natural prey, easily adaptable to our global aspirations.

For guaranteed success of such an enterprise, it is essential that civil servants working in these "offices" in the service of the State, are young, without past experience imbued with theories which we know empty and ineffective, and especially should be obsessed with the missionary spirit of the great protectors of children at risk. Because for them all parents must represent as potential criminals, potential hazards to the welfare of the child here considered to be a "God".

An "Office of Child Protection" and "Bill of Rights of the Child" have no reason to be without children at risk. In addition, the exceptions and the historical examples used for their implementation eventually sooner or later up disappearing if they were not constantly fed with new cases occurring on an ongoing basis. In this sense, we must infiltrate the "Education System" of the Nations in order to make disappear under the cover of "Modernity" and "Evolution", the teaching of Religion, History and Good Manners while diluting at the same time, under an avalanche of new experiments in the milieu of the Education, that of the language and mathematics.

In this way, by removing from the younger generations, any basis and any moral boundary, all knowledge of the past (and therefore any national pride), so all respect for others, all the power and knowledge of the language of science (and thus reality), we will help build a youth largely disposed to all forms of crime. In this new universe fragmented by the fear of parents, and their abandonment of all responsibility regarding their children, we will have a clear path to form in our own way and according to our primary objectives, a youth where arrogance, contempt, humiliation of others will be considered as a new basis of "Affirmation of Self" and "Freedom".

But we know from past experience even, that a similar youth is already doomed to self- destruction because this is fundamentally "individualistic", so an "Anarchist" by definition. In this sense, it can not possibly represent a solid basis for the continuity of any society whatsoever, and even less a sure value for the care of its elderly.

In the same vein, it is also imperative to create a "Charter of Rights and Individual Freedom" and the "Office of Citizen Protection" by dangling to the masses, that these innovations are part of the "Modernity" of the "New Societies" of the twentieth century.

In the same manner and at the same time, but at another level, to pass new laws for the "Respect and Individual Freedom". As in the case of the "Family", but on the level of the "Society", these laws will come into conflict with the rights of the Community, thereby leading the societies mentioned, right to their self-destruction. Because here, the inversion is complete: "It is no longer society (the right of the majority) that must be protected against individuals that can threaten, but rather (the Right of the Individual) which needs to be protected against the potential threats of the majority". This is the goal that we set.

To complete the breakdown of the family, the education system, thus the society in general, it is essential to encourage the "Sexual Freedom" at all levels of the Western Society. It is necessary to reduce the individual, therefore the masses, to the obsession of satisfying their primal instincts by all possible means. We know that this step represents the culmination by which any society will eventually collapse on itself. Had it not been so in the Roman Empire at its height, and similar to all civilizations throughout history?

By men of Science and the laboratories funded by our Lodges, we have managed to develop a chemical process that will revolutionize all the Western Societies, and relegate to oblivion forever, moral principles and religious Judeo-Christians. This process, in pill form, will open the way wide to the "Sexual Freedom" without consequences, and push the "Women" of the Nations to want to break with what will then be perceived as the yoke of the past (the slavery of women subjected to men and the traditional Judeo-Christian family).

Formerly "Centre and pivot of the family unit", the modern woman, now as an independent individual, wants to break with its traditional role, break away from the family and lead her life according to their own personal aspirations. Nothing more natural, we know, but where we will intervene strongly, it will be to infiltrate all the new "Feminine Protest movements" by pushing their logic to its extreme limits of consequence. And these limits can be found already registered in the definitive breakdown of the traditional family and Judeo-Christian Society.

This "Sexual liberation" will be the ultimate means by which it will be possible to us to remove the "Popular Consciousness" any reference to the "Good and to the Evil". The collapse of this religious and moral barrier will permit us to finish the process of the false "Liberation of Man's Past", but which in reality is a form of slavery that will be profitable to our "Globalists Plans".

This open door for the encouragement of "sexual freedom" to the "Divorce" to "abortion" on demand to the legal recognition of diverse forms of homosexuality will help us to radically change the historical basis of the "Legal Right" of the Societies. It be a major asset to push for all of the individuals in a general relaxation of the morals, to divide the individuals as compared against each other, according to their instincts and their own interests, to destroy the future of the youth by pushing the adverse experiences of early sexuality and the Abortions, and to break morally the future generations by pushing them to alcoholism, different drugs (which our Senior International Lodge Officers will take charge of taking the control at the world level), and in the suicide (that it be considered by a youth disillusioned and abandoned to themself, as being the chivalrous end).

Let us deceive the youth of the Nations by showing him to their parents as being irresponsible, atheistic, immoral; searching, after all, only for the pleasure, for the escape and for the wild satisfaction of their instincts at the price of the lie, the hypocrisy and the treason. Let us make of the divorce and the abortion a new social custom accepted by all. Thus encouraging him to the criminality under all the forms, and to take refuge in different groups, out of reach of the family environment that it will perceive, inevitably, as being a threat for its own survival. The social fabric being so upset for ever, it will be possible to us from then on to act on Politics and the Economic of Nations to subject them in our thank you; to come there to accept of strength, our Plans of a New World Order.

Because, it is well necessary to acknowledge, the Nations, deprived that they will be then to be able to count on a strong youth, on a Society where the individuals, grouped around a common ideal, strengthened by indestructible moral ramparts, would have been able to provide its historical support, can only than abdicate to our global will.

Thus we can then inaugurate what was so much announced by our past creations: "The communist system which prophesied a world revolution set into motion by all the rejected of the earth" and "Nazism by which we had announced a New World Order for 1000 years".

That is our ultimate goal; the work rewarded for all the valorous dead in labor for its accomplishment for centuries. Saying it loud and clear: "All the Brothers of the Lodges passed, died in the anonymity for the realization of this ideal to us is now possible to touch with the fingertips".

It is well recognized by all that the Man, once after having assured their basic needs (food, clothing and shelter), is much more inclined to be less vigilant. Let us allow him to lull his conscience while orienting to our way his mind, creating in himself pure piece of favorable economic conditions. Therefore during this period of 70 years where our agents will infiltrate all over the different spheres of the Society to accept our new standards in Education, Legal Law, Social Policy and we will make sure to spread him around an economic climate of confidence.

Labor for all, the opening of Credit for all; Leisure for all will be our bogie for the illusory creation of a new social class: the "Middle Class". Because once our objectives reached, the "Class" in the middle, between the secular poor, and we the rich, we will definitely remove by cutting off all means of survival.

This way, we shall make Nation states, the new "Parents"of the individuals. Through this reliable climate where our "International Agents" will have done what's necessary to to push aside any spectre of world war, we shall encourage the excessive "Centralization" for the State. In this way, the individuals can acquire the impression of a total freedom to explore while the legendary burden of personal liabilities will be transferred to the State.

Thus it will be possible to sharply increase the burden of the State by multiplying without any limit body of intellectual public servants. Insured for years in advance of material security, they will be consequently perfect for executors of "Governmental Authority", in other words, of our "Power".

Thus creating an impressive body of officials who in itself will form (a Government within the Government), irrespective of the political party that is in power. This anonymous machine can serve us one day means of leverages when the moment comes to accelerate the economic collapse of the Nation States, because these will not be able indefinitely sustain such mass salaries without having going into debt beyond their means.

On the other hand this same machine will give an image cold and uncaring of the government apparatus, and how this complex machine useless in many of its functions, will serve as a cover and protection against the populations. For who would dare to venture through the mazes of such a labyrinth in order to assert his personal grievances?

Always during this period of general intoxication, we shall also take advantage of it to buy or eliminate, according to the necessities of the moment, all the company directors, the persons in charge of the major Bodies of State, Centers of Scientific research among which the action and the efficiency would risk to give too much owe to the Nation states. The State should not absolutely become an independent strength in itself which would risk to escape us, and to put in danger our ancestral "Plans".

We shall also watch to have an absolute control on all the supranational structures of the Nations. These international Bodies must be placed under our absolute jurisdiction.

In the same sense, and to guarantee the profitability of our influence with the populations, we shall have to control all the News media. Our Banks will thus see to finance only those who are favorable to us whereas they will oversee the closure of the more recalcitrant. It should go almost unnoticed in principle in the populations, whom they will be absorbed by their need to make more money, and to entertain themselves.

We shall have to take care with finalizing, from now on, the phase of deregionalization of the rural regions begun at the beginning of the "Economic crisis" of 1929. Overcrowding the cities was our bedfellow of the "Industrial revolution". The rural owners, by their economic independence, their capacity to produce the basis of the food supply of the States, is a threat for us, and our future Plans. Piled up in cities, they will be more dependent on our industries to survive.

We cannot allow ourselves the existence of groups independent from our "Power". Thus let us eliminate the landowners by making of them obedient slaves of the Industries being under our control. As for others, let us allow them to get organized in Agricultural Cooperatives that our Agents will infiltrate to direct them better according to our future priorities.

Through the State, let us attempt to highlight well the compulsory "Respect" for the diversity of the "Cultures", of the "Peoples", of the "Religions", of the "Ethnic groups" which are all ways, for us, to convey the "Personal freedom" before the notion of "National Unity"; which will allow us to divide better the populations of Nation Sates, and so to weaken them in their authority, and in their capacity to maneuver. Pushed to these extreme limits but on the international plan, this concept, in the future, will urge the ethnic groups of the various Nations to group together to claim, individually, each their own part of "Power"; that will finish ruining Nations, and will make them burst in endless wars.

When Nation states will so be weakened by so much infighting, quite established on the recognition of the "rights of Minorities" in their Independence; that the nationalists divided into various cultural and religious factions will oppose blindly in fights without outcome; that the youth will have totally lost contact with its roots; then we can use the United Nations to begin to impose our New World Order.

Moreover, at that point, the "Humanitarian, Social and Historical Ideals" of the Nation States will have long since burst under pressure from the internal divisions.]

End of the 6.6.6 document.

Dated end of June 1967.

Eighteen years later, or 6.6.6. in time ($3 \times 6 = 18$ or 6.6.6.), another important meeting was held in Canada. The 6.6.6. group met again in Toronto, at the end of June 1985, but this time to finalize the last steps leading to the collapse of nation-states and the seizure of international power by the United Nations.

RED DAWN[1]

[The document: *Red Dawn*. Globalist Project Goal: establishment of the "World Occult". Means of Financing Project: Control of IMF, GATT, Brussels Commission, NATO, UN and other international organizations.]

The document:

The last eighteen years were very profitable for the progress of our world projects. I can say to you, Brothers, that we touch now almost the goal. The fall of the Nation States is not more than a question of time, relatively short, I have to admit to you confidently.

Due to our Infiltration Agents and our colossal financial resources, unprecedented progress has now been made in all areas of Science and Technology of which we control the largest corporations financially. Since secret meetings with M. de Rothchild within the 56 years, which were aimed at finalizing the development and implementation of the World "Computers", it is now

---

1   Original title: *L'aurore rouge* (1985). (Editor's note.)

possible to foresee the establishment of a kind of "International Highway" where all these machines are interconnected. Because, as you already know the direct control of individual populations of the planet at the very least would be be totally impossible without the use of computers, electronic and attaching them to each other in a vast "Global Network". These machines also have the advantage of replacing millions of people. In addition, they have neither conscience nor any moral, which is essential for the success of a project like ours. Above all, these machines do, without question, everything is dictated to them. They are perfect slaves which our predecessors have dreamed, but not that they were able to doubt that one day it would be possible to perform such a miracle. These machines without country, without color, without religion, without political affiliation, are the ultimate fulfillment of our tool and the New World Order. They are the "Cornerstone"!

The organization of these machines in a vast "World Network" the superior levers of which we shall control, will serve us to im-mobilize the populations. How?

As you know, the basic structure of our New World Order consists, in its essence, of a multitude of diverse "Networks" each covering all the spheres of the human activity on the whole of the planet. Until this day, all these "Networks" were interconnected by a common ideological base: that of the Man as being the "Center" and the "Ultimate Fulfillment" of the Universe.

So, thanks to all these "Networks" united by the link of the "New Religion of Man for Man", we were easily able to infiltrate all the human sectors in all the Western countries, and to modify the "Judeo-Christian" base. The result is that today, this Man, that it is a part of Politics, of the Economic, the Social, the Education, of the Scientific or of the Religious, already has, since our last reunion of the end of June, 67, abandoned his past inheritance to replacing it by our ideal of a World religion based only on the Man. Cut off than he is from now on from his historical roots, this Man does not wait any more, in the end, as he is proposed a new ideology. This, properly understood, is ours, that of the "Global Village Community", which will be the "Center".

And that is precisely what we will give him, encouraging him to take part, "Body and Soul", in this "Global Electronic Network" where the borders of nation-states have been forever abolished, wiped out up to their deepest roots.

While this misled man will be absorbed by his blind enthusiasm to be a part of its new "World Community" by being a part of this vast "Network of Computers", for our account, we shall see, from the superior levers which will be hidden from him, to file, to identify, to record, and to make profitable according to our own objectives.

Because inside this "New Global Society", no individual having a potential of "Profitability" for us, cannot escape us. The constant contribution of the "Electronic Technology" will have to assure us all the means to file, identify, and control all the individuals of the populations of the West. For those who do not represent "Exploitable Profitability" by ourselves, we will ensure they are eliminated through all the local civil wars that we have taken care to break out here and there through: the work of our servants; and the "Fall of the Economy" of the

Nation-States; and the "Oppositions and Claims" of various groups within those states.

Here is thus the detailed manner by which we shall proceed before 1998 to pave the road to the birth of our "World Government".

1. To multiply tenfold the "Society of the Leisure activities" which we have been so profitable to date. By serving to us as the invention of "Video" that we financed, and games which are connected with it, end up corrupting the morality of the youth. Let us offer him the possibility of satisfying now all his instincts. A being possessed by his senses and a slave of these, we know it, has neither ideal, nor internal strength to defend whatever it is. He is a

"Individualist" by nature, and represents a perfect candidate whom we can model easily according to our desires and our priorities. Moreover, remember yourselves with which ease our predecessors were able to direct all the German youth at the beginning of the century by means of the disenchantment of the latter!

2. Encourage the "Student Contesting" for all the causes connected with the "Ecology". The compulsory protection of the latter will be a main advantage when we shall have urged Nation States to exchange their "Internal Debt" for the loss of 33 % of all their territories been left to the wild state.

3. Filling in the interior vacuum of this youth by initiating him, from very young sound age, to the universe of Computers. Using that for the educational system. A slave in the service of another slave than we control.

4. On another plan, establishing "International Free Trade" as being a priority absolved for the economic survival of Nation States. This new economic conception will help us to accelerate the decline of the "Nationalists" of all the Nations; to isolate them in diverse factions, and at the deliberate moment, to set them wildly some to the others in civil wars which will finish ruining these Nations.

5. To assure us at all costs of the success of such an enterprise making sure that our Agents already infiltrated in the Ministries of Intergovernmental Affairs and Immigration of Nation States make in depth modifications to the Laws of these Ministries. These modifications will essentially aim at opening the doors of the western countries to a more and more massive immigration inside their borders (immigrations which we shall moreover have provoked by having taking care of touching off, here and there, new local conflicts). By well orchestrated press campaigns in the public opinion of Nation States targeted, we shall provoke among them a significant refugees' influx which will have the effect, to destabilize their internal economy, and to make increase the racial tensions inside their territory. We shall see to make so that groups of foreign ex-

tremists made part of these immigrants' influxes; That will facilitate the destabilization.

6. This "Free Trade" which, in reality, is not because it is already controlled by us all at the top of the economic hierarchy, infiltrating it by the "Trilateral Commission": [that of Asia, America and Europe]. It will bring us the discord inside Nation States by the increase of the unemployment connected with the restructurings of our Multinationals.

7. Shifting slowly, but certainly, our multinationals acquired in new countries to the idea of "the Market economy", such as the Eastern European countries, in Russia and in China for example. We do not care much, at the moment, if their population represents or not a vast pool of new consumers. What interests us, is to have access, first of all, to a "Workforce- Slave" (cheap and non-union) which these countries and those of the Third World are offering us. Moreover, are not their governments set up by us? Do they not rely on foreign aid, and in the loans from our "International Monetary Fund" and our "World Bank"? These transfers offer several advantages for us. They contribute to maintain these new populations in the illusion of a "Economic Liberation", a "Political Freedom" while in reality, we shall dominate them by the appetite of the earnings and a debt which they can never settle. As for the Western populations, they shall be maintained in the dream of [Economic Well Being] because the products imported from these countries do not suffer any price increase. By contrast, without them being aware at first, more and more industries will be obliged to close their doors because of the transfers that we will have conducted outside of the Western countries. These closures will increase unemployment, and will bring major losses in revenue for the Nation States.

8. So we shall set up a "Global Economy" at the world level which will escape totally the control of Nation States. This new economy will be over everything; no political or labor-union pressure can have power over it. It will dictate its own "Global Poli-

tics", and will force a political reorganization, but according to our priorities at the world level.

9. By this " Independent Economy " having only Laws as our Laws, we shall establish a "World Mass Culture". By the international control of the Television, Media, we shall establish a "New Culture", but leveled, uniform for all, without any future "Creation" avoiding us. The future artists will be in our image or will not survive. Finished therefore the times when "Independent Cultural Creations " put at any time in danger our globalist projects, like that was so often the case in past.

10. We will find it then possible to make use of the military forces of the Nation States (such as those of the United States) in humanitarian goals. In reality, these "Forces" will be used to submit our control to recalcitrant countries. Thus the Third World countries, and others like them will not be able to escape our desire to use their people as slave labor.

11. To control the world market, we shall have to divert the productivity of its first goal (free the man from the hardness of the work). We shall direct it to turn it against the man by enslaving the latter in our economic system where he will have only the choice to become our slave, and even a future criminal.

12. All these transfers abroad of our Multinationals, and the world reorganization of the economy will, among others, aim at making climb the unemployment in the western countries. This situation will be all the more practicable because at first, we shall have favored the massive import of basic products inside the Nation States and, at the same moment, we shall have overloaded these States by the exaggerated employment of their population in the production of services which they cannot pay any more. These extreme conditions will multiply by millions the masses of welfare recipients of all kinds, of illiterates, of homeless persons.

13. By the loss of millions of jobs in the primary sector, from covert evasions of foreign capital out of the Nation States, thus we will find it possible to set in danger of death the social harmony by the specter of civil war.

14. These international manipulations of the governments and the populations of Nation States will supply us the pretext to use our I.M.F to urge the western governments to set up "Budgets of Austerity" under the lid of the imaginary reduction of their "National Debt"; of the hypothetical preservation of their "International Credit rating"; of the impossible conservation of the "Social Peace".

15. By these "Emergency Budgetary Measures", we shall so break the financing of Nation States for all their "Mega-Projects" which represent a direct threat to our world control of the economy.

16. Moreover all these austerity measures will allow us to break the national wills of modern structures in the domains of the Energy, the Agriculture, the Transport and the new Technologies.

17. These same measures will offer us the ideal opportunity to establish our "Ideology of Economic Competition". This will be translated, with the Nation States, by the voluntary reduction of salaries, voluntary departures with [Presentation of Medals for Services rendered]; which will open to us doors to the establishment everywhere of our "Technology of Control". In this perspective, all these departures will be replaced by "Computers" in our service.

18. These social transformations will help us to change in depth the "Police and Military" workforce of the Nation States. Under the pretext of the necessities of the moment, and without arousing of suspicions, we shall get rid once and for all, all the individuals having a "Judeo-Christian Consciousness". This "Restructuring of the Police and Military Bodies" will allow us to dismiss without contesting, the old staff, as well as all the elements not conveying our internationalist principles. These will be replaced by young recruits devoid of "Consciousness and Morality", and

already quite entrained, and favorable to the mindless use of our "Technology of Electronic Networks".

19. In the same time, and always under the pretext of "Budgetary Cuts", we shall ensure the transfer of the military bases of the Nation States towards the United Nations organization.

20. In this perspective, we shall work on the reorganization of the "International Mandate of the United Nations". From "Peacekeeping Force" without decision-making power, we shall bring it to become a "Rapid Deployment Force" where will be merged, in a unified whole, the armed forces of the Nation states. This will allow us to carry out, without fighting, the demilitarization of all these States in a way that none of them, in the future, are not sufficiently powerful (independents) to question our "World Power".

21. To accelerate this process of transfer, we shall imply the current force of the United Nations in conflicts impossible to sort out. In this way, and by means of the Media which we control, we shall show to the populations the impotence and the uselessness of this "Force" in its current shape. The helping frustrations, and pushed to its climax at the appropriate moment, will push the populations of Nation States to beg the international authorities to form such a "Multinational Force" as soon as possible to protect at all costs the "Peace".

22. The next appearance of this global willpower of a "Multinational Military Force" will keep pace with the establishment inside the Nation States, a "Multi-Jurisdictional Task force". This combination of the "Police and Military Staff", created straight from the pretext of the increase of the growing political and social instability inside these States collapsing under the burden of the economic problems, will allow us to control better the western populations. Here, the excessive use of the identification and the electronic recording information on the individuals will supply us a complete surveillance of all the intended populations.

23. This interior and exterior police and military reorganization of Nation States will allow the convergence towards the obligation of the implementation of a "Judicial World Center". This "Center" will allow the various "Police Bodies of Nation States" to have quick access to "Data Banks" on all the potentially dangerous individuals for us on the planet. The image of a better judicial efficiency, and the more and more narrow links created and maintained with the "Military", will help us to emphasize the necessity of an "International Court" doubled by a "World Judicial System"; the one for the civil affairs and criminal individuals, and the other one for the Nations.

24. During the growth accepted by all of these new necessities, it will be imperative for us to complete as soon as possible the world control of firearms inside the territories of Nation States. To do it, we shall accelerate the "ALPHA PLAN" implemented during the 60's by some of our predecessors. This "Plan" originally aimed at two objectives which remained the same even today: by the intervention of "Crazy Shooters", create a climate of insecurity in the populations to bring to a tighter control of firearms. Direct acts of violence so as to make it appear the responsibility of religious extremists, or persons affiliated to religious allegiances of "Traditional" tendency, or still, persons claiming to have privileged communications with God. Today, to accelerate the "Control of Firearms", we can use the "Fall of the Economic Conditions" of the Nation States which will entail with it, a complete Social destabilization; thus increase of the violence. I do not need to remind you, nor to demonstrate to you, Brothers, the foundations of this "Control" of firearms. Without this one, it would become almost impossible for us to put on their knees the populations of the targeted States. Remember yourselves with which success our predecessors were able to control Germany of 1930 with the new "Laws" applied in the time; laws moreover on which are based the current Laws of Nation States for the same control.

25. The last "Stages" relate in the "OMEGA PHASE" experimented from the experiments made at the beginning of the 70's. They contain the application, at the world level, "Electro-Magnetic Weapons". The "Changes of Climate" entailing the destruction of the harvests; the bankruptcy in these conditions, farmlands; the denaturation, by artificial means of foodstuffs of regular consumption; the poisoning of the nature by an exaggerated and mindless exploitation, and the massive use of chemicals in the agriculture. All this, Brothers, will lead to the ruin assured by the food industries of Nation States. The future of the "Control of the Populations" of these States passes necessarily by the absolute control, by us, of the food production at the world level, and by the takeover of the main "Food Roads" of the planet. To do it, it is necessary to use Electro-Magnetics, among others, to destabilize the climates of the most productive States on the agricultural plan. As for the poisoning of the nature, it will be accelerated all the more as the increase of the populations will push it without restriction there.

26. The use of Electro-Magnetic cause "Earthquakes" in the most important industrial areas of the Nation States will contribute to accelerate the "Economic Fall" of the most threatening States for us; as well as to amplify the obligation of the implementation of our New World Order.

27. Who can suspect us? Who can suspect used means? Those who will dare to raise themselves up against us by broadcasting of the information as for the existence and for the contents of our "Plot", will become suspicious in the eyes of the authorities of their Nation and their population. Thanks to the disinformation, to the lie, to the hypocrisy and to the individualism which we created within the peoples of Nation States, the Man became an Enemy for the Man. So these "Independent Individuals" who are of the most dangerous for us exactly because of their "Freedom", will be considered by their fellow men as being enemies and not liberators. The slavery of the children, the plunder of the wealth of the Third World, the unemployment, the propaganda for the liberation of the drug, the exhaustion of the youth of the Nations, the ideology of the "Respect for the Personal freedom" broadcasted within the

Judeo-Christian Churches and inside the Nation States, obscurantism considered as a basis for the pride, the inter-ethnic conflicts, and our last realization: "Budgetary restrictions"; all this allows us finally to see the ancestral fulfillment of our "Dream": that of the institution of our "NEW WORLD ORDER"].

End of document.

Dated end of June 1985.

CONCLUSION

So, the "Toronto Protocols (6.6.6.)", myth or reality? It would be like asking if Brave New World is also a myth or reality even though it's a novel. Yet, its author, too, had access to "documents" of the time to create it. The author knew well that the revelation, the dissemination of the information he possessed, but in a form other than the novel, would have aroused more suspicion than acceptance among the population. And how many other authors also had to use the same stratagem to warn their contemporaries, and future generations?

So, the "Toronto Protocols (6.6.6.)", myth or reality? The urgency of the current situation, that engendered by the onset of "budgetary restrictions" marking the beginning of the end, the near realization of the "occult New World Order", did not allow for the writing of a novel (which would have taken too much time in the present context).

But the impact provoked by the revelation of these "documents" is nevertheless significant, for their publication will have the effect of placing those who originated them on the defensive.

What is desired here is that beyond the disinformation conveyed and maintained by unscrupulous politicians and people frightened at the possibility of losing personal interests, each reader can reflect, group together with others like him or her and now take measures to survive in the face of what is coming.

Even if my life is in danger because of the dissemination of information like this, yours is even more so from ignorance of this same information.[1]

So, the "Toronto Protocols (6.6.6.)", myth or reality? It's up to you to answer... It's up to you to see, in recent and future events, whether these "documents" belong to the realm of fiction or reality.

It's up to you to realize that fear has no other purpose than to paralyze you, and to place you at the mercy of those who only want to control you in order to better enslave you according to their interests which, in the end, are not yours.

Serge Monast, investigative journalist.

End of March 1995.

---

1   Serge Monast lost his life under disturbing circumstances a few months after the publication of this text (editor's note).

PUBLISHER'S NOTE

The number 666; the number of the beast in the Apocalypse of Saint John, was the subject of a very interesting study by Marc Dem, in a book published in 1996 by Rocher Publishing, under the title "666, l'Antichrist ". In it, he denounced the formidable global "telematics1" network that has been emerging for several years and whose ultimate aim can only be total control of the movements of each human being. Marc Dem also died under strange circumstances, much like Serge Monast.

TABLE OF CONTENTS

ETHOS

Éditions Ethos ®
www.editionsethos.com
contact@editionsethos.com